Horrifying True Stories: Disturbing True Tales of Murder, Mayhem and The Macabre (Horrific Crimes Book 1)

CW00486506

Horrifying True Crime Stories

Horrific Crimes

Danielle Tyning

Published by Danielle Tyning, 2020.

HORRIFYING TRUE CRIME STORIES

First edition. October 10, 2020.

Written by Danielle Tyning.

Table of Contents

Calling all true crime enthusiasts! Sign up to my newsletter for more books and stories of murder and mayhem straight to your inbox:

https://bit.ly/2zsaUup

This book is a work of non-fiction based on research by the author. It is written in British English, so US readers may find some spelling differences; for example, utilize = utilise, or color = colour.

Prologue

As someone who takes a keen interest in true crime, it feels like there's no documentary, serial killer case or horrific tale of murder and mayhem that I've not already heard of. This becomes all the more apparent when watching a *Forensic Files* episode I already know the ending of or flicking through true crime books and magazines only to be re-reading the cases I already know inside out. However, I knew there was an abundance of cases out there that I'd yet to discover - the cases that were buried, the ones that didn't receive the attention they deserved, or the ones so gruesome even the press held back on reporting about it in too much detail. These were the cases I wanted to research and write about.

With this in mind, I began delving into the most intriguing and compelling cases I'd not yet heard of and was surprised by the number of horrific crimes I'd never come across. A lot of the time I was taken aback by the sheer depravity of the murders and crimes I'll tell you about. Some were outright bizarre. Others had me wondering how we have such evil wandering the earth. Some left me questioning why we can't do more to prevent such senseless brutality from one person to another. All of them left me thinking about them for some time after researching them.

If you're intrigued by the horrifying things human beings are capable of, you've picked up the right book - *read on.*

But please be warned, the cases in this book are highly disturbing and include graphic and distressing descriptions. Please take this trigger warning seriously as this book depicts horrific crimes that involve sexual abuse, domestic abuse, child abuse and graphic violence throughout. This book intends to explore the evil in this world and expose the heinous behaviour that some people are capable of. Please heed this warning before continuing to read.

Horrifying True Crime Case #1: Rurik Jutting

The sickening rape, torture, mutilation, humiliation and murder of two Indonesian women by a British banker in Hong Kong.

Although this book mostly includes cases I've only recently stumbled upon, I have to admit I was already aware of the Rurik Jutting case before I began writing. I originally read about it in 2016 when he was convicted of the horrific rape, torture and murder of two Indonesian women in his Hong Kong apartment. However, I felt compelled to include it in this book as despite hearing about this brutal double-murder previously, I hadn't looked into it thoroughly at the time. When I came across it again while researching material for this book, I took the time to look into it a little more, just out of curiosity with no intention of including it in this publication. In doing so, I opened up a sordid world of hardcore pornography, drug abuse, extreme sexual fantasies and a sociopath spiralling out of control. Rurik Jutting reminded me of Patrick Bates from *American Psycho*; wealthy, entitled, narcissistic and harbouring a lust for blood.

The way he treated his two victims as objects rather than human beings, how he degraded them both physically and emotionally and the way he felt deserving to behave so barbaric got to me. Whilst the physical torture he inflicted upon his victims was deplorable, so were the verbal insults and baiting he used to torment his victims. We know about this because he recorded much of what he did to the two women in his

Hong Kong apartment, often facing the camera to document what was going on and to offer a sick sort of narration to the unthinkable things he was doing. In one update, he says, "It's Monday night. I've held her captive since early Saturday, I've raped her repeatedly, I tortured her, tortured her badly," and recites what he's done to his victim casually.

After I'd done my research on the case, I felt it deserved a place in *Horrifying True Crime Stories*. Delve into a story that documents a descent into sheer evil and depravity, but be warned, it's not for the faint of heart.

Rurik Jutting was born in the UK in 1985, and in his own words had a happy childhood. His loving mother chose his first name that is said to mean 'noted ruler' from its Russian origins. He described himself as an ambitious child and attended Winchester College, which is a prestigious private school. It was here he faced the disappointment of being ranked sixth in their scholarship selection, which most teens would be delighted with. However, for a young Jutting, this wasn't good enough - he wanted to be ranked first. When his mother expressed how thrilled she was at his achievement, the young boy said he found this 'almost insulting', as if she was surprised he managed to get in at all.

When Jutting was 16, his father tried to kill himself by slashing his wrists. It was Jutting who found his bloodied father, tended to his wounds, and got him to hospital. He had another traumatic experience when he said he was sexually assaulted at Winchester by another student. He was later seen by a psychiatrist who found out that Jutting had been having suicidal thoughts as well as being deeply affected by his parents' marital issues and his mother's ongoing health problems.

Despite this, the youngster was excelling academically and was accepted into Cambridge University to study history and law at their Peterhouse College. He received first-class honours for his history degree but was left disgruntled when he got a 2:1 in law, to which he blamed the examiner's approach in marking his work. This inability to accept criticism or 'failure' was an early indication of Jutting's narcissistic side.

After graduating, he went on to work for Barclays Bank, then Bank of America Merrill Lynch. He scaled the ladder rapidly, and within a few years was earning over $330,000 per year. However, living up to the 'unpredictable' moniker his manager had labelled him with, Jutting was audited in 2012 for possible violation of regulations. It was Jutting in particular who was flagged up by the auditors as being a risk to the organisation. He was then relocated to Hong Kong, which the young banker felt was a conscious decision by management to get him 'out of the way'. This relocation began Rurik Jutting's nihilistic descent into excessive drink and drug use.

By this point, he needed to drink alcohol to get to sleep. He did see a psychiatrist who he confided in about feeling down and often on the brink of tears at work. Not only did he require excessive amounts of alcohol by the time he moved to Hong Kong, but Jutting was also using cocaine to excess; so much so, on the flight to Hong Kong, he smuggled the drug in his rectum.

Beginning his new life in a new part of the world, Jutting resided at a flat in The J Residence, which is a popular area for expat workers. It offered luxury and exclusivity in a bustling area of the city. The building towered at over 41 floors, offering breathtaking views of the Hong Kong skyline at night. You could walk to the bar, the pool, or the garden of the building and get a clear view of the concrete jungle beneath you.

Despite living a luxurious life with a well-paid job, Jutting was becoming more and more melancholic. His nihilism was increasing, his social life was next to nil, and he would spend long periods alone playing video games. It was during this isolated time that he would almost obsessively delve into his lust for extreme sex, by watching sadistic pornography (known as 'hurtcore') and using sex workers. It was 2009 by this point, and his behaviour towards the women he'd hire for sex became more forceful. He began occasionally removing condoms during sex without asking, which would be constituted as rape in his native England.

At this point, Jutting was free-falling, and his life had spiralled out of control. His binges of drink and drugs would go on for days on end, causing him to miss out on important meetings at work. When he was confronted about his absence, Jutting came up with an excuse that would assure no questions were asked: he told his boss he had HIV. He needed drugs to function, he had gained a considerable amount of weight and he had pretty much stopped going to work. While he was supposed to be at work, Jutting was at home reading and watching violent pornography.

When that became stale for him, he sought excitement elsewhere. He signed up to dating app Grindr to look for men to have sex with, to which he would go on to describe the outcome of as "disappointing". He told a psychologist that he sought out sex with other men as he was "trying to do everything I could to get new experiences". However, these new experiences did nothing to pacify Jutting's lust for control and desire to inflict pain and terror on another human being. Instead, he was planning something much more brutal and sadistic.

On October 25th, 2014, Jutting got in touch with a sex worker who he'd used before. Her name was Sumarti Ningsih, and although he'd paid her for sex previously, Ms Ningsih wasn't overly keen to accept another offer from a violent Jutting. On the one occasion where they'd met before, she asked to end the session early due to her client becoming increasingly savage with her. She would give Jutting half of his money back for this session and leave roughed up, but without serious physical injuries.

However, he managed to convince her to meet up once more, where he would again beat her during sex, which quickly turned from consensual to non-consensual. Ningsih wouldn't have the opportunity to end the session early on this occasion, as she would never leave his flat alive, despite her begging and pleading with Jutting to let her go.

She would be held captive by a drug-fuelled madman who tortured her using a number of implements, including pliers, sex toys, his belt, and his bare hands. He mutilated the young woman as he taunted and bullied her continuously. In one of the many phone recordings of his murderous bender, he is heard saying to Ningsih, "Do you like the fist?" as he torments her by pushing her genitals. "It's better than being beaten, right?" he asks her. He went on to threaten to cut off her nipples, telling her he would get her some water after "just one more", presumably referring to "one more" bout of abuse.

He would go on to describe his sick acts of degradation, telling the camera, "I've never seen anyone that scared. She voluntarily ate faeces out of the toilet... and then just smiled at me afterwards." Revelling in the control he had over his victim, Jutting continued, "I urinated into her mouth. She threw up and I made her eat her own vomit. I made her take drugs."

He would also film parts of the physical torture on his phone, then proceed to offer lengthy narrations of the things he'd just done to his helpless victim. In one sick confession, he said he beat her genitalia so badly she "bled from her labia". He would use cocaine throughout the relentless torture of Ms Ningsih, claiming to drift in and out of the influence of drugs. He claimed to have become "quite apologetic" to his victim when he was "less under the influence of cocaine" and told the young woman repeatedly that he loved her. Regardless, on day three, he killed her.

He made her kneel in front of his toilet and lick the bowl. Her hands were tied behind her back. She did as she was told, and in her final moments, she was degraded, terrified and compliant in the hope she would escape with her life. Sadly, releasing her was never on Jutting's agenda. As she was hunched over the toilet bowl, hands bound, he cut her throat. This wouldn't be the end of her suffering, however, as she didn't die straight away. Jutting would then drag her into the shower to finish what he started.

Once she had died, her sadistic killer would wrap her up and bundle her small frame into a suitcase, leaving it on his balcony.

Jutting hadn't been to work in the fortnight leading up to his drink, drugs and murder binge, but after killing Ningsih, he changed the wording of his out-of-office to, *For urgent inquiries, please contact someone who isn't an insane psychopath.* He continued his bizarre message by saying, *For escalation, please contact God, although suspect the devil will have custody.* He followed this up by saying the last line (about the devil having custody) would only be relevant if he has "followed through". It seems as though Jutting was, at this point at least, considering suicide after he was done with his killing spree.

He also resumed filming himself explaining what he'd done and how he felt. In one recording, he says, "It felt really good. Yeah, it's good. I reduced her to a sex object. Then I realised, hang on, this is actually not that difficult or bad." He continued, "After I already beat her so badly, told her her life was over... that I was going to rape her repeatedly and kill her... even after that she wanted to live."

The murder of Ningsih didn't satisfy Jutting's lust for rape and torture, and on October 31st, he began his sinister plans for victim number two. He went out and equipped himself with a torture kit which included a blow torch, sandpaper and nails. He filmed his newly acquired 'kit' on his phone while offering a monologue as to how he could use his tools on his victim. After stocking up his torture tools, he went out that evening to catch his "prey", Seneng Mujiasih. It was Jutting himself who referred to his victim this way, telling police, "I was hunting for prey and she was, unfortunately, the person who was hunted."

Upon meeting Mujiasih, he invited her back to his place for sex. She agreed and went back to his apartment, where the pair began cuddling and kissing on his sofa - but not before Mujiasih sent a text to her friend complaining about the "really bad" smell inside the apartment. This, as we now know, would have been the decomposing body of Sumarti Ningsih. By this point, she would have been on the balcony for around five days. This session didn't last too long, however, as the young woman spotted a gag nearby. Panicked, Mujiasih let Jutting know she'd seen the gag and began shouting at him; the killer didn't take too kindly to this reaction and held a knife to her throat. Jutting told her he would kill her if she kept struggling, which didn't stop her from trying to get out of his grasp. Angered by her lack of compliance, he sliced her neck.

After this second killing, he resumed his cocaine binge. He also continued the commentary of his crimes on his phone, saying that killing Mujiasih "may have been kindness," moving the camera towards his own genitals while saying, "living with that would have haunted her."

Again, despite the horrific acts he'd just carried out, work was still on his mind. He called his boss and told him he was in big trouble, telling him that he would need to do something in order to protect the reputation of the bank. He eventually called the authorities, deciding not to follow through with his plan of ending his own life.

When the police arrived, they found Mujiasih and soon discovered the naked woman laying on the floor was dead. She had wounds to her buttocks and neck. They arrested Jutting but didn't immediately find the body in the suitcase on his balcony; Ningsih would remain in the suitcase for a few more hours until police fully searched the property.

Investigators found 43 videos on the killer's phone, which were played at his trial (to which he pled not guilty to murder on the grounds of diminished responsibility). He would go on to plead guilty to manslaughter, but that would be rejected by the prosecution. The jury at his trial was shown videos of the victims being tortured as well as Jutting's lengthy camera-facing, narcissistic narration. The jury had individual screens of the torture footage to stop the press from being able to view it, although they could still hear the haunting audio of the victims' screams and Jutting's vile threats, such as, "Do you want me to hit you? If you say 'Yes', I hit you once. If you say 'No' I hit you twice". Between drug binges and torture sessions, Jutting spoke about returning to the UK to kidnap teenage students and force them to be his sex slave. While this was being shown on the screen playing the video, Jutting looked away. While there was no empathy or remorse shown from him, he at least seemed to feel some shame about his self-important ramblings to the camera.

The clips of him admitting to the murders, plus the overwhelming amount of violent footage on his phone was enough to ensure the jury found him guilty of murder. In November of 2016, he was sentenced to life in prison. Since then, he appealed for a re-trial, blaming the judge in his original trial for the life sentence he received. He argued that Michael Stuart-Moore, deputy judge, had narrowed down the scope of the defence argument by stating that only a psychiatric disorder would be constituted as an "abnormality of mind". Jutting's lawyer, Gerard McCoy, said that his client showed extreme traits of psychiatric disorders that go way beyond the normal range. Because of this, McCoy argued that Jutting was not in control of his actions when he tortured and killed his victims. His retrial request was quickly shut down.

In the aftermath of Jutting's trial, Sumarti Ningsih's father spoke out to say his daughter had called him a few days before she was murdered. Chillingly, during that conversation, the young woman told her father that "Rurik Jutting was haunting her". She said the Brit wanted to force her to marry him, adding that Jutting often wanted to "kidnap her". Her parents are now the caretaker of Ningsih's child.

I believe the true depravity and violence of this case have been somewhat concealed from the public and the facts and evidence available have been made purposely limited. Even so, the crimes of Rurik Jutting stayed with me long after reading about them. What his victims went through in their final hours is incomprehensible, and I strongly get the impression that there's little remorse from Jutting for the atrocities he committed.

Horrifying True Crime Case #2: Issei Sagawa

While living in Paris in 1981, Issei Sagawa killed and cannibalised a Dutch woman. He was released after just two years of pre-trial detention. He walks the streets a free man to this day despite still harbouring the urge to eat human flesh again.

When you're young, you enjoy playing with your friends and spending your time taking advantage of the freedom of childhood. However, when Issei Sagawa was a little boy, he enjoyed nothing more than daydreaming about *eating* his young playmates.

He says that in the first grade, he looked down at his own short and skinny legs that "looked like pencils". He then noticed a classmate's thighs and thought they looked "delicious". He looked to the media's representation of Western women such as Grace Kelly and says this is what sparked his cannibalistic fantasies, comparing it with what the majority of us would call sexual desire. Whereas others would admire beauty and dream of looking like Hollywood stars, Sagawa dreamed of eating them. He maintains that he never thought of killing another human at this point, only wanting to "gnaw" on their flesh.

Born on 26 April 1949 in Hyogo Prefecture to wealthy parents, Sagawa was a sickly child. He was born prematurely and was said to have been small enough to fit in his father's palm. Soon after birth, he developed enteritis, a small intestine disease.

Although Sagawa would eventually recover from this, his fragile health led him towards developing an introverted personality. His contained and introspective persona saw him develop a keen interest in literature. This would stay with him as he grew older, and despite harbouring urges to consume another person, his younger years right up until his early twenties passed by without any controversial or criminal behaviour. That would last until he was 24, and at university in Tokyo.

It was here that Sagawa followed a German woman home and broke into her apartment as she was sleeping. His intent after breaking in was to cannibalise her by slicing off part of her buttocks then take off with her stolen flesh to eat it. However, his victim woke up mid-attack and fought him off. Sagawa was detained by police and charged with attempted rape, as he didn't confess his true intentions to the authorities when questioned - he preferred to accept the rape allegation rather than admit his cannibalistic cravings. The charges of attempted rape were eventually dropped when Sagawa's father paid a settlement to the woman.

In 1977, three years later, Sagawa moved to Paris to study literature at the public research university, Sorbonne. It was here, he said, that his cannibalistic urges began to overwhelm him. He would recall that during his time there, almost every night he would bring a prostitute home and try to kill them. He'd hold a gun up behind their head while they were blissfully unaware of the danger they were in. However, he would always freeze up when the time came to pull the trigger. He admitted that this ritual of sorts wasn't just about eating his victim, but rather it developed into an obsession to carry out the killing of a girl.

It wasn't Sagawa's conscience that stopped him from pulling the trigger each time he had the chance nor was he having a change of mind about what he was doing. Each of the prostitutes he returned home with were destined for death - and then to be cut up and consumed - but Sagawa says it was pure "instinct" that stopped him going through with this plan. He says, "The world that I lived in would shatter to pieces the moment I pulled that trigger," and this stopped him in his tracks each time. The thought of his own world collapsing prevented him from killing, not the thought of the victim or what their families would endure in the aftermath of their murder.

His craving to kill and eat another human being wouldn't stay contained for long and he soon found the perfect victim. She studied at the same university as Sagawa and was in one of his classes. The young woman was friendly and warm to Sagawa, which is a stark contrast to his experiences with the French women he was surrounded with. The self-described "short and ugly" man with an inferiority complex struggled to interact and connect with his female peers and would acknowledge they were out of his league. However, he knew there was something different about fellow student Renee Hartevelt and soon struck up a friendship with the young woman.

Soon the pair would become close and Sagawa would occasionally invite Hartevelt over for dinner. As their friendship blossomed, the young students' trust in her soon-to-be killer would grow too. Sagawa would prepare sukiyaki - a hotpot - for the pair at his house. He says it was on this occasion he began to see the young woman as having real potential to be his victim; the one he would murder in order to consume her flesh. He would later say, "The moment I saw her wash her hands in the bathroom, the image overlapped with the prostitutes washing at the bidet in my mind, and inevitably she became another candidate for my 'ritual'".

This would trigger an obsession for Sagawa. From that moment on, every time he met Hartevelt he would point his gun at her from behind. Still, he continued to freeze when it came to pulling the trigger and pointing his gun at an unbeknown Hartevelt became something of a ritualistic act. Despite numerous failed attempts at shooting his friend, the certainty that he was going to kill her eventually wasn't ever in question - it was just a case of *when* he would go through with it.

In an interview with Vice magazine in 2009, Sagawa recalled his frame of mind during this time, saying, "One day, one of the employees from my father's company came to Paris and took me to a Japanese restaurant. I had a bit of a fever that day, which might have made me delusional because the whole time I was thinking about how she was coming over the next day, and how if I got food poisoning from the raw fish that I ate there, I wouldn't be able to finally realise the fantasy that I'd been obsessing about for 32 years."

The next day he held the gun up behind Renee Hartevelt's head and pulled the trigger. After years of pent up yearning to kill and eat another being - a woman - Sagawa had finally taken the leap from dark fantasy to morbid reality. However, the gun misfired and Hartevelt was unharmed.

For most people who found themselves crossing a line like this, the gun malfunctioning could serve as a snap back to reality; to make them see how wrong their actions are and how severe and senseless ending an innocent woman's life is. However, the mishap with the gun didn't deter Sagawa; in fact, it made him somewhat hysterical. Now more than ever, he knew he needed to kill his friend. Two days later, dangerously unaware of just how lucky she'd been a few nights prior having left with her life intact, she returned to Sagawa's house. He again crept up on her from behind, held the gun to her head and pulled the trigger. The bullet wasn't powerful enough to go right through the skull, so instead, it spun around in her head, killing her.

Overwhelmed, Sagawa looked down at the bloodied woman on the floor and thought about calling an ambulance. However, he soon shook any feelings of guilt or empathy out of his mind and reassured himself he'd done the right thing - he'd been dreaming of this day for over three decades and now it was finally here. It would be stupid of him to call an ambulance now. No way would he sabotage his dreams now.

Sagawa abused the corpse in the worst ways you can imagine. He raped Hartevelt over the course of several days. He tried to bite her flesh to eat her, but it became apparent that his teeth weren't sharp enough to tear her apart like he wanted.

He went out and bought a butcher knife to properly dissect his victim. He ate her face and breasts, sometimes raw, sometimes cooked. Parts he didn't consume were kept in the fridge for later. Talking about the aftermath of murdering his friend, Sagawa said, "The first thing I did was cut into her buttock. No matter how deep I cut, all I saw was the fat beneath the skin. The moment I saw the meat, I tore a chunk off with my fingers and threw it into my mouth. It was truly a historical moment for me."

Sagawa documented his crime by taking pictures of Hartevelt's body throughout his eating of her, showing her in various stages of having been cut up by him. The murderer did feel some remorse about his actions by this point - he was regretful that he hadn't eaten his victim alive. "What I truly wished was to eat her living flesh," Sagawa would later say.

After a few days, Sagawa had eaten (or frozen for later) most of her pelvic region, so he put what was left of Hartevelt's legs, torso and head into two suitcases and jumped into a taxi. He was dropped off at the Bois de Boulogne park, where he intended to drop the suitcases filled with body parts in the secluded lake nearby. His plan to go unnoticed was foiled by his own carelessness as several people noticed that his suitcases were dripping with blood. The French police were quickly notified of this and Sagawa, clutching his suitcases filled with limbs, was apprehended. When questioned by police, his response was honest yet jarring: "I killed her to eat her flesh," he would bluntly confess.

Sagawa's father's wealth afforded him to hire a top lawyer for his son's defence. After being held for two years awaiting his trial, Sagawa would be found legally insane and as a result, would be declared unfit to stand trial. He was ordered to be held indefinitely in a mental institution. It was while he was in the institution that he received a visit from author Inuhiko Yomota. As a result of this meeting, Sagawa's own account of his crimes was published in his native Japan entitled 'In the Fog'. This led to Sagawa achieving somewhat of a macabre celebrity status back home where he was deported to by order of the French authorities. He was committed to Matsuzawa Hospital in Tokyo where his examining psychologists unanimously declared him sane, stating that sexual perversion was the sole motivation for the murder of Hartevelt.

By this point, the charges against Sagawa in France had been dropped. The court documents were sealed and were never submitted to the Japanese authorities and as a result, there were no grounds to legally detain Sagawa in Japan - they had no reason (on paper at least) to keep him there. Sagawa was free to check himself out of the hospital whenever he wanted, which he did on 12 August 1986. He's remained a free man since then.

Sagawa is now something of a minor celebrity in Japan. He has often been invited to be a guest speaker or commentator for television programs and has penned reviews for magazines. In 1992, he appeared in an exploitation film called Unfaithful Wife: Shameful Torture (which was an exploitation film). His role in the movie was as a sadosexual voyeur. Sagawa had also penned books about the murder he committed, and he wrote a commentary book about the Kobe children's serial killings in Japan of 1997. His story has inspired multiple songs and films, including the Rolling Stones song 'Too Much Blood'. Sagawa was also documented on the History Channel show called 'Strange Rituals' discussing cannibalism, where the programme showed Sagawa as a successful freelance artist of nude paintings.

Horrifying True Crime Case #3: The Murder of Katarzyna Zowada

Katarzyna Zowada was believed to have been skinned alive by her murderer to make a 'skin-suit'.

There's very little information out there in regards to this case, but after reading about it I was intrigued enough to delve deeper and find out as much as I could about the murder of Katarzyna. Her disappearance and her death were shrouded in mystery and it's hard to think about how cruel and painful her last moments alive were. The murder is still being looked into by Polish police, despite them having jailed Robert Janczewski for the killing, and it seems they're reluctant to offer any details about the crime. Regardless, I've pieced together the scraps of information available to create a timeline of this disturbing case.

Katarzyna Zowada was a 23-year old-studying of Religious Studies at University in Krakow, Poland. Katarzyna was said to have been a pleasant young woman, but according to those who knew her, she suffered from depression. They described her as being "sad and withdrawn" which ties in with her attempted suicide leading her to receive psychiatric treatment. Her reclusiveness meant she spent most of her time alone and it's been noted she didn't have many friends around. Her time was mostly spent at home with her mother.

Along with her mother, Katarzyna was due to attend an appointment at the psychiatric hospital on 12th November 1998, but she never turned up. Her mother was immediately concerned, given her daughter's history of mental health issues. Straight away, she reported her daughter missing to the police, worried that she'd hurt herself once more. Her mother was told they couldn't file a missing person report yet just and advised her to wait.

On 6th January 1999, two months after Katarzyna had gone missing, the crew of the Elk pusher boat were on the River Vistula when they stumbled upon an odd-looking material wrapped around the propeller of the boat. The strange material was pale in colour and had a pungent, foul smell when you approached it. Upon closer inspection, the crew found what they thought looked like a human ear attached to the unfamiliar material. The authorities were immediately notified and it was taken to a lab to be tested where the worst-case scenario was confirmed: the material was human skin. The DNA identification also confirmed the skin belonged to Katarzyna, with forensics noting that it had been in the water for around 2-3 weeks before it was found.

Just over a week later, on 14th January 1999, Katarzyna's right leg was recovered in the River Vistula. Despite searches, only her right leg, her skin and a few shredded articles of clothing of hers were ever found. Her other limbs and face were never discovered. From the evidence retrieved and further examination of it, it was revealed that Katarzyna's flesh had been turned into a suit of skin, which was speculated to have been worn by her murderer. This possibility reminds me of Ed

Gein, who tried to create a 'woman suit' from human skin in the hopes of literally "crawling in her skin". However, unlike Gein, the killer in this case likely didn't remove the human skin from a corpse - it's more probable was done while the victim was still alive.

Analysis by forensics concluded that the skin had been very carefully removed between Katarzyna's thighs and neck and, in the torso region, her nipples were missing. There was no skin from Katarzyna's face or arms present on the suit, with the flesh suit only going up as far as her left ear. Despite it not being totally clear if Katarzyna was skinned while she was alive (although this is the most likely scenario) or if she was already dead before her skin was removed, it was suggested at the time that she had been tortured prior to death.

For years there were no leads or arrests on this case, which probably wasn't helped by the fact that there was little investigation into her disappearance before her skin was found. Considering this crime was committed in the 90s, and mental illness wasn't viewed in the same way it is today, it's possible that authorities could have taken the case less seriously as if it were a mentally-well missing young woman. As there was no sense of urgency to find Katarzyna when she initially vanished, most of the evidence that could have led police to her was long gone.

In yet another disturbing twist, soon after finding Katarzyna, the forensic medicine unit in Krakow received a corpse with a scalped head. The killer turned out to be the victim's son, Vladimir, who'd been spotted wearing a mask made of human skin. The mask was later revealed to be that of his victim - his own father's face. As you'd expect, this made investigators take a closer look at Vladimir as a possible suspect in the murder of Katarzyna; however, they could find nothing to link him to the crime. He was charged with his father's murder and received 25 years behind bars.

For years, the case remained incredibly cold, although in 2014 the FBI representative for Europe outlined a profile for the killer, noting he had sadistic tendencies. Two years later, it was confirmed that Katarzyna had been tortured before she was killed - as was previously suspected - and that her murderer was likely trained in martial arts.

More years passed and the case was still chilly, with it looking as if there'd never be an arrest made for the crime that was committed decades prior. Then in October 2017, Robert Janczewski was arrested, 19 years after Katarzyna was brutally murdered. Janczewski had initially been a person of interest in 1999 when the case was still somewhat fresh, but there wasn't enough evidence at the time to connect him to the murder. By 2017, however, the evidence had accumulated to the point where police had enough to charge him with aggravated murder.

Janczewski fit the profile police were looking for; he was trained in martial arts, had known the victim, had visited her grave and had a history of harassment towards women. He was also sadistic, which was another trait the profiler said belonged to the suspect. He had previously worked at the Institute of Zoology, where one day he killed all of their rabbits, resulting in his termination of employment. He offered no explanation as to why he did this. It's here where he would have picked up knowledge on skinning animals, which is something he could have transferred over to the skinning of a human.

Janczewski was detained after police obtained a letter to him from a friend. The content of this letter remains undisclosed, as do a lot of the details of this case, but it was enough to tie him to the murder of Katarzyna. When he was arrested, police searched his property and found blood in his bathroom and a journal in which he'd allegedly written about the murder. While being held in jail as investigators gathered more evidence, Janczewski would complain of harassment from the prison guards. After this was investigated and found to be groundless, 'lying to police' was added to his rap sheet. He's also been charged with aggravated murder alongside particular cruelty and remains behind bars as the case is investigated further.

The case of Robert Janczewski was hard to uncover as there's little information available due to Polish police classifying the case and ensuring little to no details are released to the public. However, I'm keen to see that Katarzyna finally gets the justice she deserves, so I'll be keeping a lookout for updates on this case.

Horrifying True Crime Case #4: Jerry Brudos

Jerry Brudos was an American serial killer and necrophile who committed the murders of at least four women in Oregon.

Despite my interest in true crime, I'd never really looked into the Jerry Brudos case in too much depth. I'd heard of the 'shoe fetish killer' before, but I'd never really educated myself about him or looked into the details of the crime. When I delved into the case and researched it in all its gruesome detail, I knew it deserved a place in this book. It's in equal parts horrifying and terrifying that he managed to get away with his crimes for a number of years.

Jerry Brudos was five-years-old when he was playing in a junkyard and stumbled upon a woman's spike-heeled shoe. It was the first time he'd come close to seeing such a thing, and he was immediately in awe of it. It was a singular shoe and it's matching foot was nowhere to be seen; nevertheless, the youngster was immediately fascinated with his find. He swiftly brought the shoe home with him and kept it in his room. This chance discovery would be the beginning of a lifelong infatuation with women's shoes. Throughout his childhood, Brudos would try to steal shoes from his teachers as well as his mother in order to satisfy his growing fetish. This childhood obsession would grow into something more deadly and sinister as Brudos got older. What could have remained a harmless sexual fetish rapidly grew into something nobody could predict.

It's been reported that Brudos' mother was resentful of her child. When the boy was born, she already had one little boy, and she had hoped for a girl throughout her second pregnancy. The disappointment she felt when Brudos was born developed into resentment for her child as the years passed. Her hostility towards her second son would be something that would continue for the rest of her life.

She would discover her son's fascination with women's shoes by catching him wearing them while he was alone in his room. Upon discovering a young Brudos in stilettos, she immediately snatched the shoes from the young boy and quickly destroyed them, leaving the boy feeling rejected, and possibly triggering a future hatred for his sexuality. His mother would repeatedly reject the youngster emotionally, and the fact that she had repressed his sexuality (albeit possibly unintentionally - the era was very sexually repressive and it's likely most mothers would have reacted to their son's shoe-wearing in a similar manner) caused hatred to manifest inside Brudos. What would begin as hatred towards his mother would eventually twist itself into to nasty, full-blown case of violent thoughts, misogyny and disturbing fantasies.

As he entered his teen years, he began breaking into the houses of neighbours with the intention of stealing their underwear to add to his growing collection. By this point, his sexual fantasies had turned uber violent. Jerry would be 17-years-old when he attacked a woman for the very first time. Despite being inexperienced in abduction and acting out his violent thoughts, Brudos' first foray into attacking the opposite sex was especially brutal; he had a knife and used it to coax a teenage girl into posing naked while he took pictures of her. There are slightly different versions of events, but he is reported to have beaten and threatened her if she didn't comply with his demands. Despite the brutality, the young woman escaped with her life, and Brudos and was arrested for assault. As a result, he would be sent to Oregon State Hospital and kept in the psychiatric ward for nine months. While he lived here, he was still allowed to attend school throughout the day. After undergoing psychiatric evaluation, he was diagnosed with schizophrenia. It was noted that his rage was aimed primarily towards his mother. As such, he was released with the suggestion that he live a more independent life away from his mother, and he initially followed this advice. He graduated from school, going on to become a mechanical and electrical engineer. Some time was served in the military, but he would later be discharged, apparently due to his odd fetishes that were frowned upon.

Now a 22-year old man, Brudos began a relationship with a 17-year old girl from Salem, Oregon, who he would go on to marry. He moved to Portland and was living (from the outside looking in, at least) a 'normal' life. However, the dark urges within him hadn't been quashed. His stint in the psychiatric ward had done little to rid him of his violent fetishes, and he would use his new bride to act out his sexual fantasies. He would have her clean the house naked, all the while he was taking pictures of his nude wife as she carried out her chores. It remains unclear whether or not this behaviour was forced by Brudos or a consensual act between the pair, but various reports indicate that the young wife was somewhat brainwashed by her husband. Her complicity began to wane after a few years and she stopped being intimate with her husband. His fixation with wearing women's underwear around the home and his obsession with women's footwear became too much for her.

In 1967, Brudos would go on to attack his second (known) victim. He was walking downtown when a pair of high heeled shoes caught his attention. He was fascinated, intrigued and aroused by the shoes, and promptly followed the woman wearing them home. He waited for her to go to bed and broke into her house. He strangled her until she was unconscious and proceeded to rape the helpless woman. When he was done acting out his sexual fantasy, he picked up the shoes she was wearing when he spotted her and left with his trophy.

He managed to stifle is dark urges for another year, but his lust for something more than rape wouldn't be held down much longer. Rape would escalate to murder, and it would occur without much planning from Brudos. As we'll see from his murderous crimes, he was something of a chancer when it came to acquiring his victims.

Young, budding saleswoman Linda Slawson sold encyclopaedias door-to-door. In January 1968, the pretty 19-year old would knock on Brudos' door. It would be a fatal chance encounter, as the man pretended to be interested in what she was selling and invited her into the house. Once he lured the woman in under the pretence of buying her wares, he strangled her to death, but not before beating her with a ply of wood. What's so shocking and brazen about this is the fact that his mother and children were in the house as he lured the young saleswoman to his basement. Once he was sure she was dead, he proceeded to dress her in various female undergarments and place stolen shoes on her feet. As he was dressing her up, he would pose her in a number of provocative ways as he interchanged his victim from different shoes and underwear. When this wasn't enough, he took a hacksaw to her left foot and preserved it in a freezer. It would be used to model his growing collection of women's high heel shoes. Surplus to his sick requirements, Linda Slawson's body would be disposed of in the Willamette River.

To avoid her finding his collection of trophies, Brudos told his wife not to venture into the attic or garage without asking him first. If he was in there and she needed to enter, she was required to ask his permission via an intercom system. Little did his wife know, Brudos was just beginning his 18-month spree of rape, murder, and acting out his dark fantasies.

His next victim, 18-year old Karen Sprinkler, was kidnapped by Brudos while he was dressed in women's clothes. She encountered the murderer in a parking lot of a department store where he would hold the young woman at gunpoint and usher her back to his garage. He forced her to try on his collection of women's underwear as he again posed her while taking pictures of her. He proceeded to rape her and then strangled her to death by hanging her by her neck from a pulley. Following the callous murder, Brudos would go on to have sex with her dead body on a number of occasions and would cut off her breasts in order to make plastic moulds of them. Again, when he was done, the dead body was thrown into the Willamette River, tied to a car engine.

That November, he would add another victim - and more trophies - to his list of depravity. 23-year-old Jan Whitney had broken down on Interstate 5 (between Salem and Albany) and was stranded by her car. Brudos happened to be passing by and saw another opportunity to act out his sick fantasies. He offered to drive the young woman to his house and told her he would let her call a tow truck from there. Whitney agreed, trusting the helpful man, and jumped into Brudos' car. Whilst in the car, he brought out a leather strap and strangled her, proceeding to rape Whitney in the vehicle after she had died. He returned home with the dead body and carried her to his garage where he would hang her from the pulley. Again, he molested, dressed up and had sex with the corpse, and as he did with Karen Sprinkler, he cut off a breast - just the one this time. He made a mould of it and used it as a paperweight.

When Whitney was no longer of use to him, Brudos threw her in his usual dumping ground, this time tied to a piece of railroad iron. On this occasion, he also threw in Slawson's decayed foot in the river after it had rotted to the point of being useless.

His next two attempts at acquiring victims thankfully failed. He tried to kidnap Sharon Wood at gunpoint from a parking garage in the spring of 1969. Around the same time, he also tried to abduct 15-year old Gloria Smith - again he failed. 22-year old Linda Salee wouldn't be so lucky. Mere days after his failed attempts at abduction, he snared Salee from a shopping mall parking lot and took her to his garage. Yet again, he raped her and would tamper with her corpse, but this time decided against cutting off her breasts; he decided that they were 'too pink'. Still, murder, rape and necrophilia weren't quite enough to satisfy Brudos, and he decided to try and make the dead body come alive and 'jump' by driving an electrical current through the lifeless corpse. His experiment failed, and once Brudos was done, the young woman was subsequently tied to a car transmission and thrown into the Willamette River.

It would become almost a ritual for Brudos to then dress up in high heels after a murder and masturbate.

One month after the abduction of Salee, a fisherman would find a body bobbing in the water of the river as he was seeking out fishing locations. He informed the police of his morbid find, and two days later the cops would find another body in the same location. The two bodies were mutilated, and both had been tied to car parts in an attempt to make them sink to the bottom of the river. Frustratingly for the police, the river had washed away practically all of the evidence, but they did have some leads that would prove vital; some students at

Oregon State University reported receiving calls from an odd man who claimed to be a Vietnam veteran looking for a date. With not much else in the way of evidence, police looked into this further.

One girl, in particular, had met up with this 'Vietnam veteran', but had decided against pursuing anything more after feeling strange around the odd man. Somewhat clutching at straws but hopeful in finding some kind of real lead, they persuaded the girl to arrange another date with the older man. Jerry Brudos arrived to pick up his date and found the police waiting for him and he was detained.

After he was identified by a previous assault victim in a line-up, police were granted a warrant to search his home; the evidence they would find would be damning. Amongst the hoards of evidence was nylon rope, the sick trophies he had kept from his victims and the pictures he would take of their dead bodies in various poses.

Police proceeded to interrogate him, and Brudos confessed to the murders and abhorrent crimes he had committed. He even admitted to the assaults and attempted kidnappings he had not been captured for. Despite confessing to Slawson's murder, he would never be tried for this crime due to lack of evidence.

In June 1969, Brudos pleaded guilty to three first-degree murders - the Sprinkler, Whitney and Salee killings. He was given three consecutive life terms of imprisonment. Whilst in prison, the killer would collect piles of women's shoe catalogues which he kept in his cell. His reasoning for this is that they were simply a substitute for pornography magazines.

Despite being found guilty, and admitting his guilt, Brudos didn't use his time in jail to reflect or try to feel remorse for his sick crimes. In one of his many appeals, he would claim that a photo taken of him with one of his victims' dead bodies was not proof of his guilt because it was not the body of the person he was convicted of murdering - despite admitting his guilt to this earlier.

The parole board in 1995 advised Brudos that he would never be released from prison. This turned out to be true, as in March 2006, after 37 years in jail, he died of liver cancer.

Horrifying True Crime Case #5: David Parker Ray

David Parker Ray is a convicted kidnapper, rapist and suspected serial killer who tortured his victims in a self-made 'Toy-Box' using a variety of tools and implements.

Kidnapper, torturer and serial rapist David Parker Ray is suspected of murdering dozens upon dozens of women - up to as many as 60 - throughout his sick criminal career. The bodies of these women were never found, so he was never actually convicted of murder, but the evidence against Parker Ray is undeniably overwhelming.

The story of the Toy-Box Killer - as he was dubbed due to the 'Toy-Box' he held his victims captive in - goes beyond what most of us can comprehend another human is capable of doing to another.

In March 1999, Cynthia Vigil, a 22-year old prostitute, was looking for clients in a parking lot in Albuquerque, New Mexico. The young woman was approached by an undercover police officer. He told her that she was under arrest for soliciting and swiftly got Cynthia in the back of his car after handcuffing her. However, the man who apprehended Cynthia was actually David Parker Ray, and he wasn't driving her to the police station at all - he was driving her to his nearby trailer. Unbeknown to Cynthia, she was on her way to his soundproofed, makeshift torture den - his Toy-Box.

After bundling the young woman into his self-made chamber of pain, he chained her to the table in the centre of the trailer. It was similar to the type of chair you would find at the gynaecologist. Upon seeing this cold contraption, alongside Parker Ray's other torture tools, you can only imagine the sheer fear and panic that Cynthia would have been feeling as she was strapped down and restrained on the table.

For the next three days, along with his accomplice and girlfriend Cindy Hendy, Parker Ray raped and tortured the helpless young woman. The heartless pair would torment Cynthia using electric shocks, medical instruments, whips and sex toys. Prior to her ordeal, a tape was played for Cynthia - much like you see in the *Saw* films where Jigsaw plays a video recording for his victims before exposing them to the pain he has in store for them. This recording would detail exactly what her fate would be and what kind of pain she was going to endure. You can only try to imagine how frightening it would be to hear the torture you're going to be subjected to while being strapped down, unable to do anything about the pain you're about to face.

In this ominous cassette recording, Parker Ray explained to his victim that she should only refer to him as "master". He also stipulated that she should refer to the woman accompanying him as "mistress". She was forbidden from speaking unless she was spoken to first. After outlining the house rules, Parker Ray chillingly went on to describe exactly how he would torture and rape his victim. He said Cynthia would never see her family again, and told her he would "kill her like the others", clearly letting his terrified victim know that she wasn't the first and likely wouldn't be the last. He was letting her know he'd gotten away with murder before - and he was going to get away with it again.

On day three of her ordeal, Cynthia was left alone with just Hendy. Parker Ray was at work but trusted his accomplice to ensure that their victim would remain restrained and subdued until he returned. However, Hendy appeared to become complacent and left the keys to Cynthia's restraints on top of the table near where she was chained. The young woman saw her opportunity to escape and grabbed it with both hands. With sheer grit and determination, she lunged towards the keys glistening just feet away from her and was able to release herself from her shackles. Hendy returned to find Cynthia free from her restraints and tried to stop her from escaping, but she didn't bank on the broken victim having so much fight left in her. Cynthia stabbed Hendy in the neck with an ice pick and bolted out of the trailer wearing nothing but a slave collar and padlocked chains.

Desperate, bloodied, frightened but with adrenaline running through her veins, she banged on the door of a nearby mobile home, praying that they would answer. Fortunately, the owners were home and they brought the hysterical woman inside their house and called the police. Parker Ray and Hendy were swiftly arrested.

After this arrest, the police obtained a warrant to search his home and the torture trailer - the *Toy-Box* - and they would be disturbed by what they would find.

As they entered, they encountered the gynaecologist-style table. There was a mirror mounted on the wall above this so the victims would have to watch the vile and painful torture they were enuring. The horrors didn't end there; scattered throughout the Toy-Box were clamps, surgical blades, chains, saws, sex toys, whips, and leg spreader bars. Frighteningly, there was a contraption made out of wood that had been utilised to bend over and immobilise Parker Ray's victims so he could rape them.

The walls were littered with intricately detailed diagrams showing different techniques used to inflict unimaginable pain on his victims.

Also in the Toy-Box, police uncovered a videotape made in 1996. It depicted a clearly terrified and distressed woman being raped and tortured by Parker Ray and his accomplice girlfriend.

Quickly news of Parker Ray, his girlfriend and their sickening crimes became public, which prompted another woman to come forward with an eerily similar story. Her name was Angelica Montano, and she was an acquaintance of Parker Ray. She recalled how she visited his house for cake mix, only to be drugged, tortured and raped before being dumped on a highway in the blistering desert. Despite being found like this by police, there was never an initial follow up and this case. You can only wonder how many victims would have been spared should Montano's case have been thoroughly investigated at the time.

However, it could also have been that the victim had very little tangible information to give the police; after all, Parker Ray would use drugs on his victims in order to induce memory loss and amnesia. Sodium pentothal and phenobarbital were often his drugs of choice. They ensured victims would have great difficulty in remembering what happened to them.

Montano's coming forward with her story only served to strengthen the case against Parker Ray as they now had two victims with similar stories testifying against him; not to mention the abundance of incriminating evidence found in his Toy-Box. Hendy, the willing accomplice, quickly folded when police questioned her. She offered up everything she knew about the murders and pointed them in the direction of two more accomplices: Parker Ray's own daughter, and another friend named Dennis Yancy. Police quickly swooped in on the pair.

Yancy would admit to taking part in the killing of another victim, Marie Parker. He confessed to strangling her to death after she was drugged, raped and tortured by Parker Ray and his daughter.

Police were rapidly gathering more and more evidence and information, and in their attempt to discover the identities of other unidentified victims, they released some details about the woman in the videotape. She was eventually identified as Kelli Garrett, who turned out to be an ex-friend of Parker Ray's daughter.

Nicknamed 'Jessie', Parker Ray's daughter was playing pool in a saloon with Garrett in July 1996. Jessie proceeded to place a roofie in Garrett's beer, allowing her to become subdued enough for her father to place a collar and lead on her and bring her to the Toy-Box. For the next two days, Garrett was subjected to vile rapes, torture and persistent drugging. After her two days were up and she was no longer required or of use, Parker Ray looked to end his victim's life by slitting her throat. He callously sliced her neck and dumped her at the side of a road to bleed out. However, by some miracle, the young woman survived. Frustratingly, no one believed her story; not the police or even her husband. On the contrary, her husband believed she was at fault and accused her of cheating on him whilst she was being restrained, raped, and tortured by Parker Ray in his Toy-Box. Her husband subsequently filed for divorce that same year.

The drugs that Garrett had been forced to consume had made sure she was limited in what she could tell the police, and her recollection was foggy at best, but she did recall clearly that she was raped by "the Toy-Box killer". Sadly, as well as the drugs, the socioeconomic status of many of Parker Ray's victims made it difficult for their stories to be heard, accepted and believed by jurors. On top of this, the killer wasn't ever going to go down without a fight - he had too much of an ego and so little respect for his victims to offer them an acknowledgement of his crimes. He even managed to beat two of the cases put against him.

Regardless, the Toy-Box Killer was eventually sentenced to 224 years in prison for multiple offences involving abduction, sexual torture and rape. His daughter received 9 years in jail and his accomplice Cindy Hendy received 36 years behind bars.

As I mentioned earlier, David Parker Ray is suspected of committing many more offences than the ones he was eventually convicted of. This is corroborated by the abundance of evidence found in his torture trailer; there was evidence of numerous murders, including diaries penned by Parker Ray himself in which he details the murders of at least 50 women. It's not beyond the realms of possibility that he would have gotten away with this many murders - after all he chose vulnerable victims, and the ones who managed to get away with their lives intact struggled to recollect what had happened to them. Even Hendy and Yancy told police of areas in which they believed Parker Ray had disposed of bodies, although no human remains were ever found in these places.

David Parker Ray died on May 28th 2002 of a heart attack. He was just three years into his life sentence spanning over two centuries.

I always feel a huge sense of injustice when a criminal like Parker Ray finally gets apprehended and then they die without serving the jail term they were handed and most certainly deserved. The only saving grace here is that there's no chance of him ever hurting anyone ever again.

Horrifying True Crime Case #6: Nicholas John Crilley

The sickening tale of a Queensland man who raped, burned and beat a woman so severely over a 23-day period that paramedics thought she was dead when she was eventually rescued.

In 2017, Brisbane amateur rugby league player Nicholas John Crilley carried out a near-fatal, brutal and prolonged attack on his victim, a 22-year-old woman. The victim, who was described as his girlfriend, still remains anonymous to the public. However, after the sustained and horrific torture she endured, she has spoken out to say she'll never be the same again emotionally or physically. Crilley disfigured his victim so badly she says she feels she's stared at every time she leaves her house. During my research, I managed to find out her identity, but to respect her desire for anonymity, I'll refrain from mentioning it in this book.

Nicholas Crilley held his victim for a total of 23 days, abusing her horrifically, raping her, torturing her and setting her on fire. Upon reading about this sick three-week reign of terror and torture, my immediate thought was, *why?* The more I looked into this and sought out the rationale - however senseless and absurd it would have been - for the cruel campaign of violence towards this young woman, the more I realised there was no answer to the question why; he did it simply because he wanted to. Control, power, and a lust for extreme violence are all motivators in this crime, although they don't fully unveil the answer to why he did it.

The events that led up to the kidnap and torture of the young woman has been mostly kept under wraps, as have many of the surrounding details regarding the case. After researching the newspaper reports, court transcripts and the victim testimony, I managed to compile the timeline of the sick rampage Crilley embarked on.

On July 2nd, 2017 in Bulimba, a suburb in the City of Brisbane, Queensland, police attended a property after receiving a call stating a woman was there and in "pretty bad shape". The caller certainly wasn't wrong.

When police arrived, they discovered the decomposing body of a young woman, stuck to a blood-stained, dirty mattress on the floor. She had burns all over her body, tissue was falling off her face and it was infested with maggots. Severe injuries covered the entire length of her body. The stench was unbearable; there was no doubt that this was a dead body. The police likened the sight to someone who had been in an explosion. Then, unbelievably, the lifeless woman let out a helpless moan; she was alive, barely. Paramedics were immediately called and the woman was rushed to hospital in critical condition.

At the hospital, it was discovered she had a broken nose, extensive burns to her body, a broken eye socket, broken ribs and chemical burns to her throat. She also had a hole on the side of her head. These sickening injuries helped piece together the past three weeks of torture she had endured at the hands of Nicholas Crilley. From boiling water to acetone to his cigarette lighter, Crilley seemed hell-bent on utilising various methods to severely burn his victim.

Prosecutor Sandra Cuprina said of Crilley that he "subjected the woman to severe physical, psychological and sadistic violence". She went on to describe how he would sexually assault her daily, and his beatings and torture of her were relentless and severe. He would set her on fire for his own amusement and poured scalding hot boiling water onto her genitals. During beating his victim, Crilley would become sexually aroused and rape her.

The woman, by this point immobile due to her injuries, beaten both physically and mentally, was also forced by her sick captor to eat her own vomit and faeces. A testament to his depravity and savage nature, Crilley demanded that his victim should choose her own means of death; either he shot her or she died in a car crash. Unbelievably, Crilley hadn't kept his violent crime to himself - at least one of his friends knew what was going on. And, even more unbelievably, his friend did nothing at all about it. Jeromy Lee Harris, an ex-pro soccer player, was living with Crilley while the abuse was taking place at his two-story home. He knew all about the woman in the bedroom who was suffering unimaginable pain, humiliation, and torture, yet decided not to do anything to prevent it. As the saying goes, *the worst people on Earth are not only those who commit evil but those who stand by and turn a blind eye.*

The torture not only occurred at his home, but Crilley had also taken the woman to Spring Hill's Tower Mill Metro Hotel, where he hid his victim for five days. He then transferred her broken body back to his home where he continued his sick routine of burning the woman before proceeding to head upstairs to take drugs afterwards. The judge at his trial would describe this as Crilley's 'pattern' of behaviour - that he would spend hours burning his victim, then take drugs. He would then return back to her for intercourse (as the judge referred to it).

It emerged at the trial that Crilley bragged to his friend, "I've pummelled her so hard, she can't talk anymore". He was right - he'd beaten her so severely that her upper lip had detached from her face. He continued his witless bragging by saying, "I poured methylated spirits onto her and set her alight, I have pummeled her so hard I think she's had a stroke". The deep lacerations to her face became badly infected over the course of her 23 days in captivity, being mercilessly beaten. The 46% of her body that was burnt would eventually cause degloving of the skin.

The near-fatally injured woman would have died if police hadn't received a phone call on July 2nd alerting them to the barely-alive body at Crilley's residence. It was Crilley himself who made the phone call, but he neglected to mention that he was the one to cause the horrifying injuries, and told the operator that he 'didn't know what happened to her'. He then fled his property. It would be eight more days before police apprehended him, but not before a hot pursuit in which he stole a number of vehicles in order to evade capture.

There was no way Crilley could defend himself or his actions; his victim, although critical, was alive. There was CCTV evidence showing him bundling the woman from Spring Hill's Tower Mill Metro Hotel. There was ample evidence at his property where he carried out the bulk of his depraved acts.

The monster had finally been caught, but not before he'd managed to carry out one of the most depraved, meth-induced, violent crimes I've heard of. Doctors had to place his victim in an induced coma and she would spend eight weeks in the hospital recovering. The abuse she endured was so severe that her rehab included learning to speak, eat and walk again.

Understandably, she continues to suffer psychologically with PTSD and flashbacks. Her face remains disfigured, and she has an abundance of scarring all over her body from the brutal beatings and severe burns she suffered during her three weeks being held captive.

Crilley's defence at his trial would argue that his triple zero call ultimately saved the young woman's life, but the judge quashed this and ruled that the call was only made because Crilley cared about one person - himself. "Your anonymous call undoubtedly led to the (woman's) life being saved," the Judge told Crilley. "That is not necessarily an indication of remorse. Your treatment of the (woman) was callous and cruel," he continued.

The victim bravely gave her own statement at the trial, telling the court her ordeal is something she wouldn't wish upon her worst enemies.

Crilley was convicted of a total of 62 offences, including supplying a dangerous drug, 18 counts of rape, sexual assault, GBH, serious assault, deprivation of liberty and torture.

"Your brutality took her to the edge of death. The victim's life will never be the same," the Judge said as she handed Crilley five life sentences of 15 years and terms of up to 25 years' imprisonment for the rape offences. He was given a further two life sentences of 15 years for two counts of malicious acts with intent.

Crilley was already familiar with prison life before this conviction as he'd been in jail previously for assault and drug related offences. In 2014, he set himself upon a woman and her boyfriend at a McDonalds, grabbing the woman by the wrists with what was described as 'extreme force', and pulled her around violently. He proceeded to throw food at her which hit her in the face. The assault began when Crilley was said to have made unwanted advances to the woman (who was there with her boyfriend) before he began verbally abusing the pair and assaulting the victim. For this, he was sentenced to 100 hours of community service but was made to come back to court a year later, for neglecting to finish his service. For this he was subsequently jailed.

I find it hard to comprehend this crime. Even though Crilley was high on drugs for the majority of his three-week crime spree, there must have been sober moments of clarity - even the most callous of criminals are prone to bouts of empathy. However, even when the drugs (which was something Crilley had blamed his evil actions on) had worn off, he still kept his victim hostage and abused her. There was no remorse, no pangs of conscience, not even a small amount of regard for the woman he was repeatedly, mercilessly torturing. His previous crimes towards women indictate to me that he has a severe problem with them, a hatred or disdain which manifested iteself into the prolonged and vicious torture of his victim in 2017. The severity of this crime makes me wonder if that kind of contempt can ever be cured.

Horrifying True Crime Case #7: Donald Collins

Robbie Middleton, on his eighth birthday in 1998, was tied to a tree, doused in gasoline, and set on fire. Twelve years later, he eventually succumbed to his extensive injuries, but not before finally naming his attacker. It was a boy who had sexually assaulted him two weeks before setting him alight.

The most frustrating cases of horrific crime or murder are the ones where the victim never receives justice or they have to live a life of suffering without ever seeing their tormentor receive their just deserts. This case was undeniably frustrating for me to research, not only because the victim of this crime was only eight, but because he survived with devastating injuries (both mental and physical) for years. He eventually succumbed to his horrific injuries - burns to 99% of his body - 13 years after he was savagely attacked. This is the story of the murder of Robbie Middleton and the events that led to the eventual capture of his killer, Don Collins.

It was a sweltering hot day in Splendora, Texas on the 28th of June, 1998. It was also the birthday of little Robbie Middleton, who woke up excited about turning eight and was looking forward to buying new things with his birthday money.

He bought fireworks and planned on walking through the woods behind his house which connected the Crossno neighbourhood. This is where his friend lived and Robbie was going to set up a tent in his backyard (one of his birthday gifts) and have his friend camp out with him. His mother pitched the tent up for him that day, recalling that, "It was really, truly one of the happiest days of his life. He just really loved his birthdays."

On this scorching afternoon, which should have been a day of laughter and celebration, Robbie was horrendously attacked in the woods as he walked to his friend's home. He was bound by rope to a tree before being drenched in gasoline and set on fire. When the rope burned through, Robbie was free to fall from the tree. It was then he bravely managed to get his way home in a cloud of burning flames, collapsing in the street. His mother Colleen would be the one to discover her son, burnt, blistered and barely clinging to life.

Straight away, Robbie was dashed to the hospital. He'd suffered third-degree burns to 99% of his tiny frame. Only one part of his body had remained untouched - the soles of his feet. His parents were devastated to be told that he wouldn't survive. But by some miracle, he did.

After the attack, Robbie named his attacker as 13-year-old Donald Collins. Donald was known as a local sexual predator, despite his young age. He lived near the Middleton family and Colleen had often warned young Robbie not to go near Donald. She told her son to run away if he was ever playing alone and saw the dangerous teenager nearby. Donald was arrested for the horrific attack and would go on to spend several months in juvenile detention. However, he was soon released due to lack of evidence and police not being able to find a motivation for him to commit the crime.

After the attack, Robbie endured over 200 operations including skin grafts. Despite going through so much trauma and pain, he was optimistic and looked forward to putting the horrific events behind him and moving on. "The past is the past. You need to let it go," Robbie would say. However, despite his abundance of hope, his organs were incredibly damaged by the fire and in 2011, Robbie passed away from cancer that was inflicted by the horrific burn injuries. The cause of his death would be ruled a homicide.

17 days before he passed away, Robbie did something to help him get justice for the suffering he'd endured for so long. He made a 27-minute video in which he named Donald as his attacker yet again. This time, however, Robbie had more information to reveal that would shock everyone. He divulged that two weeks prior to the shocking attack, Donald had raped him in the woods (where he would later go on to set him alight). After over a decade of injustice, a motivation was finally revealed.

"He pulled my clothes down and started raping me,'" Robbie said, revisiting the painful memory of the attack. Although revelaing this secret was no doubt difficult for Robbie to do, it finally gave police the missing motive they needed. To help corroborate these new allegations, three years after his assault on Robbie, Donald had been convicted of sexually assaulting another young boy.

Robbie went on to describe how he had been walking through the woods when the teenager crept up behind him and hurled gas in his face. "Don grabbed me by my shoulder and threw gas in my face, after that I don't really remember anything," recalled Robbie. He explained how he managed to stumble through the woods and get onto the public road near his house. Robbie also revealed that as he was on fire, he also heard the voice of an adult who was talking to Donald.

After Robbie's death and his video admission, Donald was arrested and charged as an adult with capital murder. At the time of the attack, the culprit had to be at least 14 to be tried as an adult. However, years later, that had changed. Donald's defence argued that moving the case to an adult court would violate Donald's rights as the law in 1998 didn't allow him to be tried as an adult. However, prosecutors said that the murder didn't take place until 2011 at which point minors as young as 10 could be put on trial as an adult.

During the trial, Colleen told the courtroom that Robbie's final weeks on earth had been spent worrying that he would end up in hell for eternity. He was so worried about the afterlife that he refused to watch much more than children's cartoons out of fear it would show something sinful or racy. "You're the best person I know," his mother would comfort him. "You're not going to go to hell, Robert."

Gordon Pranger, who met Robbie during his ongoing recovery, said that Robbie had confided in him that he was worried about going to hell because he'd been raped. "Even though he didn't have a choice in it happening, I think that he felt that

that was a sin of having sex before marriage," recalled Gordon. Several witnesses would also testify that Donald had admitted to them that he was responsible for the savage attack on Robbie. The little boy that Donald had sexually assaulted after Robbie also testified, saying that after assaulting him, Donald had threatened to burn him if he ever spoke about it.

Heather Marie White also testified. Her mother was married to Donald's cousin, and she said that Donald had confessed to her that "him and Rex hurt Robbie". Rex was Donald's uncle. Questions had been swirling for years about his potential involvement in the crime. He would deny the accusations and prosecutors didn't take it further as they said they didn't believe that he was involved. However, with Robbie saying he heard an adult's voice, it does seem fitting that Donald could have had an accomplice; Robbie's family firmly believed that an adult was also involved in the attack on the youngster. 'I absolutely believe there was an adult on the trail. But Mr Collins won't ever tell who it was,' Robbie's mother would say.

A jury convicted Donald of murder in 2015. He was sentenced to a maximum of 40 years. The predator was finally apprehended for his crime thanks to Robbie, who managed to find some sort of justice, even after he'd died.

Horrifying True Crime Case #8: Shelly Knotek

Dubbed 'America's Most Evil Mother', Michelle 'Shelly' Knotek is a convicted murderer who tortured and killed lodgers who she welcomed into the family home. She also abused her young daughters, beating them and locking them in kennels or chicken coops as punishments.

The case of the Knotek's fell under my radar despite my huge interest in true crime. I'm not sure how, particularly as this case was made somewhat mainstream after a book dedicated to the events that occurred in the Knotek home was released in late 2019. Still, I only learned the ins and outs of this case when doing my research for this book. Although I find this case undeniably shocking, I'm afraid to say I don't think it's that uncommon as a theme in society; a family hiding sinister truths behind a veneer of 'perfect' family life. To be clear, I don't think this is the case for every seemingly perfect family, and I certainly don't think such families are hiding anything as extreme as multiple murders (like the Knoteks were), but this case did cement the idea in my mind that we never really know what's going on behind closed doors. Quite the opposite in fact, especially when people make it their mission to create a facade that no-one would ever question the validity of. This case is horrifying for many reasons: the violence exhibited by mother-of-three Shelly, who severely abused those she ought to protect. The weight of the manipulation and fear that Shelly used in order to evade justice for so long. The untimely deaths of three people and the scarred lives of the children that witnessed those murders. For me, the idea that Shelly could be so cruel, controlling and callous while holding up the appearance of being a perfect mother and family woman really gave me something to think about.

From the outside looking in, they were the epitome of idyllic family life; living in the charming city of Raymond, Washington, the family of five were well-presented, living a comfortable life and appeared to dote on one another. Shelly appeared to be happily married to David, a hard-working man who strived to provide for his family by working long hours at his construction job. Shelly had two daughters, Nikki and Sami, before meeting David, who he treated like his own. The pair went on to marry in 1987 before they had a daughter together named Tori in 1989.

As the children got older, Shelly and David began to offer their home out to those less fortunate or who'd fallen on hard times. Just before Tori was born, the couple took in Shane Watson, Shelly's 13-year-old nephew. Later that same year, Shelly's friend Kathy Loreno also moved in with the Knotek family after losing her job. If we jump a decade later to the early noughties, the family then also took in US military veteran Ron Woodworth after he lost his home. On the surface, you see a warmhearted family unit that takes it upon themselves to help those in need by offering a roof over their heads when they're in dire straits. However, not all was not as it seemed.

If you looked a little deeper, it became apparent that the Knoteks' house guests disappeared one by one. It wasn't exactly clear where their former lodgers had gone or what had happened to them - Shelly only ever offered up opaque reasons for their sudden disappearance to any family or friends who asked. She'd tell them that they'd run away or decided to move to a different town for a job.

But Shelly was lying. She knew exactly what had happened to Shane, Kathy and Ron. She had cut each of them off from their family and friends and subjected them to a prolonged campaign of terror, abusing them all physically and emotionally before murdering them. She took advantage of the people who'd turned to her when they were in the most vulnerable times of their lives, offering them a false sense of hope.

The horrific stories of the victims remained undiscovered until 2003 when the Knotek girls got in touch with the local sheriff's office and unburdened themselves of the horrors they'd kept secret for so long. The truth about what had gone on in the family home was finally revealed and the Knotek children could ensure their mother was finally brought to justice. The story of this seemingly perfect family was eventually laid bare and Shelly was exposed as the cold, callous murderer she was.

When Shelly met David in a bar in April 1982, he thought she was "the most beautiful girl" he'd ever laid eyes on. However, even in the early stages of the relationship, it was clear to David it was unhealthy. Shelly wouldn't hesitate in verbally abusing him, slapping him and assaulting him. Despite David knowing deep down that the relationship was abnormal, his submissiveness prevented him from standing up to her. As well as being subservient to Shelly, David adored his wife and didn't dare confront her about her treatment of him for fear of reprisal. Instead, he chose to turn a blind eye to the violence. David's submissiveness escalated from 'turning a blind eye' to actively participating in violence as time went by and became his wife's willing accomplice in her morbid crimes.

Once the Knotek's two older daughters - whose respective fathers are believed to have left the family unit due to their mother's manipulative behaviour – reached their tween years, they too fell victim to Shelly's mistreatment and sadistic ways. She would force her girls and their lodger relative, Shane, to stand outside in freezing cold temperatures while naked. To add extra pain and humiliation to the youngsters, Shelly would go out of her way to douse them with ice-cold water as they stood in the stinging cold. Callous Shelly called this punishment "wallowing" and it was doled out for 'crimes' like visiting the bathroom without asking.

Shane had moved in with the Knotek's because his father was in and out of prison and was pretty much absent from his son's life (even when he was out of jail). He was a member of a biker gang and chose the lifestyle that accompanied it over providing a stable home for his son. His mother struggled with substance abuse and wasn't able or willing to meet her teenage son's needs. In pursuit of the stable, loving home he craved so much, Shane sought out his relative, Shelly. Being her nephew, he had no reason to hesitate when Shelly offered him a roof over his head. She would go on to betray his trust in the worst ways; she invited him into her home with the promise of stability and lured him in with the hope of a better future. Instead of following through on those promises, Shelly would mercilessly torture and abuse Shane and would eventually go on to murder the young man.

Shelly cruelly bullied her older girls by forcing them to snip off tufts of their pubic hair in order to embarrass them. She would laugh wickedly when her daughters reluctantly obliged to her humiliating demand and would bask in their upset and shame. In other emotionally abusive instances, Shelly also forced Nikki and Shane to dance together naked. The teens, as any young adult would be, were thoroughly mortified by this degradation.

Shelly would also take to locking her children in the kennel or chicken coop as a form of punishment. Sami, the middle child, was attacked by her mother on such a regular basis that the young girl always wore trousers to hide her bruises from school teachers. The eldest, Nikki, received much of the same treatment from her mother. During a school holiday, she threw a teenage Nikki head-first through a glass door, blaming her daughter for the violence she was enduring by shouting at her, "Look what you made me do". Despite her daughter's face dripping with blood, Shelly felt it necessary to remind her child the beating was her own fault for acting up.

Shelly would tend to her daughters' wounds instead of seeking proper medical help in order to make sure she wasn't exposed as the violent, abusive parent she was. For the most part, she would inflict injuries that weren't easily visible and that could be concealed with the right clothing. This emotional and physical abuse would be offset by the mother intermittently showering the youngsters with adoration and affection. Not only did this serve to somewhat win back the children's trust, but it also helped her fool outsiders and conceal the reality of Knotek family life. Shelly ensured her girls always wore the best clothes and had the must-have possessions, which in turn made them popular at school.

Kathy Loreno, who was an old friend of Shelly's, was certainly fooled by the false good samaritan and perfect mother charade. 30-year-old Loreno, who was a witness at Shelly's wedding to David, moved in with the Knotek family in winter 1988, a few months after the family had taken Shane in. At first, the Knotek's kept up their pleasant and respectable front, warmly welcoming Loreno into the fold. The new lodger would show her gratitude by helping Shelly with the children and doing chores around the house. For a short while at least, this setup worked well for the family and their newfound guest.

This masquerade would quickly dissolve, however, as Shelly soon started to berate, abuse and beat her friend. Progressively the abuse worsened to the point that Loreno was forced to work naked, was fed sedatives and made to sleep in the basement next to the boiler. If she were to leave the house with the family for whatever reason, it would be in the boot of the car, not in the passenger seat even if one were available. This abuse lasted six years, primarily at the hands of Shelly Knotek.

Thin, frail and the shell of the person she was before residing with the Knotek's, Loreno managed to survive six years at the hands of Shelly and David. Sadly, in 1994, following an especially prolonged and brutal beating from Shelly, Kathy Loreno died. Without conscience or remorse, her killer quickly summoned her husband, daughters and nephew to issue them a stern warning: "All of us will be in jail if anyone finds out what happened to Kathy." Ever the faithful aide, David later burned the body to dispose of any evidence of Loreno's sadistic demise.

To cover up the horrific truth, Shelly told Loreno's family that the former hairdresser had run away with her boyfriend named 'Rocky' and was deliberately vague when answering any questions they asked about her whereabouts. Despite the Loreno family not fully believing Shelly's story, they had no option but to accept her version of events as there was no tangible proof to suggest anything otherwise. A private investigator hired by Loreno's brother advised him that she had probably been killed by Shelly Knotek, but with no evidence, their hands were tied.

After the murder, Shane had something he wanted to show Nikki in the hope of finally bringing his murderous relative to justice. He took Nikki to one side and showed her something he'd been keeping a secret - photographs that he'd covertly taken of Kathy in her most distressing moments. His Polaroids showed the woman naked, beaten black and blue and crawling along the floor. Shane had taken these pictures with the intent of taking them to the police, confiding in Nikki in the hope that his relative would join him and back up his story. However, his intent to expose the house of horrors to the world was brought to an abrupt end. To this day, Nikki still finds it difficult to explain what she did next. After Shane divulged his plan to her, she went to her mother and told her that Shane was hiding the incriminating pictures in a teddy. I can only imagine that Nikki didn't expect the following events to unravel as they did.

In February 1995, at the instruction of Shelly, David fired a bullet into Shane's head. By this point, he was 19-years-old and had lived with the Knotek's since he was 13. He'd been like a son to David, despite the abuse and violence the teenager had endured throughout the last six years of his life. Much like Kathy Loreno, Shane's body was burned by David to dispose of the evidence. His remains were scattered in the ocean.

Shelly told the children that Shane had gone to Alaska where he'd found work as a fisherman and maintained this manufactured story for years, even going as far as to falsify instances of contact from their relative. Oddly, David even went as far as missing work on a few occasions to go on "searches" for Shane, which obviously ended up being unsuccessful. However, these searches did achieve one thing: it ensured that the Knotek girls believed that their father was trying his hardest to find Shane, throwing them off the scent of what had really happened to the missing teen.

The family then took in another lodger in the early noughties, a local man in his 50's named Ron Woodworth. Described as witty, the easy-going veteran had been friendly with the Knoteks for years before he moved in with them. Like clockwork, it wasn't long before Shelly's sadistic cycle of emotional and physical abuse started again.

As with Kathy Loreno, the matriarch began by verbally abusing Ron, telling him he was worthless and disgusting. This vile treatment of him soon moved on to harsh beatings. Just like her first victim, she also drugged Ron with pills and withheld his basic needs. She'd restrict food, clean clothes and prohibit the use of the indoor bathroom. As she was upping the abuse, Shelly would set out to estrange him from his friends and family in her bid for complete control and power over her victim. Witnesses would later describe seeing Ron being forced to do chores outside in only his underwear, and also recalled a time when he was made to jump from the family's second-story roof onto the gravel below with nothing on his feet. This caused broken bones and severe wounding on his legs. It was also claimed from witnesses that Shelly would burn Ron's injured feet with bleach and scalding water.

Ron succumbed to his many injuries and died in August 2003, aged 57, after four years of abuse and suffering at the Knotek house. Seasoned manipulator Shelly lied to the handful of people that remained in Ron's life by telling them he'd moved away after he got a new job. She even went as far as applying for a change of address on his credit card, changing it to Tacoma, Washington.

By this point, Tori was only 14-years-old and was the only sister still living at the family home. She had nobody to talk to about the abuse and violence that was going on within those four walls and turned to her sisters Nikki and Sami to confide in them about Ron suddenly going missing. The two elder sisters were now in their 20s and had moved to different parts of Washington State, and despite no longer being among the abuse on a daily basis, their gut told them that Ron hadn't merely vanished. They were convinced that their mother was responsible for whatever had happened to him and they tasked Tori with looking for evidence to support their theory. The teen did as she was asked and quickly discovered a pile of Ron's possessions in an outhouse alongside some bloody bandages. Finally, the sisters had the evidence they needed and had summoned the courage to go to the authorities and tell them everything that had gone on in the Knotek house of horrors.

They called the police who discovered Ron's body buried on the Knotek property. An autopsy couldn't confirm the exact cause of Ron's death when his emaciated body was eventually unearthed, although it was covered in an abundance of burns and bruises. Immediately, Tori was removed from her parents' custody and was placed in Sami's care.

Kathy's body was never located, but David would later confess that he'd been the one to dispose of her remains. After his arrest, he also confessed to shooting Shane and burning his corpse at the family home. Shelly was charged with two counts of first-degree murder for the deaths of Kathy and Ron, and David was charged with first-degree murder for his slaying of

Shane. Both of them accepted plea deals for lesser charges, which saw Shelly allowed a rare Alford plea, which enabled her to plead guilty to the charges while still asserting her innocence.

By doing this, she prevented a trial that would've aired all of the atrocities that occurred in the Knotek household to the public. Even after being caught, it seems Shelly was adamant that she'd retain as much control as she could. It was revealed that all three of the Knotek's late victims had tried to run away from the abusive home, but Shelly managed to hunt them down, and manipulate them into going back to the house of horrors. Recounting this story to someone else, their question to me was, "Why did all of the victims go back when they could have escaped?" To me, this is a testament to just how manipulative and controlling Shelly was - she could abuse her victims in the most horrific ways, yet when they were so close to freedom, she still managed to maintain enough power over them to coerce them back.

David served a total of 13 years behind bars for second-degree murder, the unlawful disposal of human remains and rendering criminal assistance and was released in 2016. Shelly is scheduled for an early release back into society in 2022. She'll have served 19 years in prison for second-degree murder and manslaughter.

The Knotek girls have gone on to carve out successful lives for themselves, working hard to forge promising careers and building homes for themselves far removed from the one they grew up in. The sisters are close and have no contact with their mother but remain terrified of what might happen upon her looming release from prison. They're not sure whether she'll try to get in touch with them or seek out more vulnerable victims. The latter is certainly a danger as it seems prison hasn't managed to rid Shelly of her need to control and manipulate, as she's reportedly been using her powers of influence to exploit her fellow prisoners; so much so, she's no longer allowed to share a cell.

The Knotek case served to remind me that not only can monsters often live in plain sight, but they also might not be as far away as you think. In this case, they were the typical family next door.

Horrifying True Crime Case #9: The Hello Kitty Murder

In Hong Kong in 1999, a nightclub hostess was kidnapped and tortured in an apartment in after stealing a wallet. She would eventually die from the injuries she sustained at the hands of her attackers.

Hello Kitty and the word 'murder' doesn't fit together naturally. Hello Kitty is a fictional, cutesy character that was created in Japan and has made its way around the world to become a cult icon. The character has spawned merchandise, a TV show, clothing, comics, video games and even a themed restaurant. The brand certainly doesn't have any sinister or dark ties - apart from the case of Fan Man-yee.

This chilling tale of rape, torture, and murder is named after the Hello Kitty doll the victims' severed head was hidden inside of.

This gruesome crime occurred in 1999 in Hong Kong. Fan Man-yee was a nightclub hostess, and at 23, she had her whole life ahead of her. Despite her young age, she'd had a tough life right up until her untimely death. After being abandoned by her parents as a youngster, she was raised in a girl's home. As she entered her teen years, prostitution became a way of funding her growing drug habit, which she eventually became dependant on.

Although her life was addled with addiction, Fan got herself a job as a nightclub hostess which led to her selling her body for money in order to fund her dependency on drugs. It was a vicious cycle she was unable to get out of. While working at the nightclub, she met 34-year-old Chan Man-lok. He was a socialite, pimp, and a drug dealer - and Fan was just the type of person he knew he could exploit. It didn't take long for the pair to become friendly and soon Man-lok had added Fan to his inner circle.

Despite their apparent closeness, Fan was still battling drug addiction, and when she needed money for her next fix, she stole Man-lok's wallet. Fan took off with about $4,000 from the stolen wallet. It was a crime she would pay for with her life.

Man-lok and his 13-year-old 'girlfriend' - along with accomplices Leung Shing-cho and Leung Wai-lun - would carry out a month-long reign of imprisonment, torture, terror, and rape upon Fan in retaliation for the wallet stealing. The group did unimaginable things to the young woman; she was bound, burned, beaten, and forced to do sickening things for the groups' sadistic amusement.

Using electrical wire, Fan's wrists were tied together and she was suspended from the ceiling. While she hung, the group used metal pipes and table legs to repeatedly strike Fan until she was a pulp of blood and broken bones. They melted plastic and dripped the scalding hot liquid onto her. Chilli oil would then be rubbed into her painful burn wounds, causing excruciating suffering. They also urinated in her mouth and even forced her to eat Man-lok's girlfriend's faeces.

The horrific torture Fan endured lasted an entire month before she succumbed to her injuries and died.

Whilst the entire case is undeniably senseless, what makes this even more unfathomable is that Fan had already paid Man-lok his money back - with added interest. When it was discovered she'd stolen the money, it was demanded that Fan pay it back with $10,000 interest, which she did. Man-lok then decided that this wasn't enough, and demanded even more money from Fan, which she was unable to obtain. As a result, Man-lok and his group took it upon themselves to kidnap and torture the young woman.

Fan fought to live for a month until her body gave up on her.

When she was found dead by one of the evil group, they decided to cut her body up with a saw. Once dismembered, she was spared just as little dignity in death as she was in life. The gang cooked her body parts on the stove, using the same utensils to stir their own dinner as they used to stir Fan's boiling body parts. All of Fan's remains were then disposed of in the rubbish, apart from one body part: her head.

This was crudely placed inside a Hello Kitty mermaid toy.

It's thought that this horrific crime would have gone unpunished (and some would say the crime still has gone properly unpunished) if Man-lok's girlfriend hadn't felt haunted by the crime she witnessed and participated in. The teenage girl began to feel like Fan was haunting her, and believed her restless spirit wasn't going to leave her alone unless she went to the police to confess. The teen did take herself to the police station to exorcise herself of the ghost that had been haunting her, but the police initially rejected her story as a sick fantasy. *Something so disturbing and horrific couldn't be true, right?*

The police eventually did search the premises where Fan's life tragically ended, and it corroborated with the youngster's version of events.

Surprisingly, despite all of the evidence and Man-lok's former girlfriend testifying against them, no one was charged with the murder of Fan. The three men involved denied murder, although they did admit stopping a lawful burial from taking place. During the trial, the trio all placed the blame on each other for the most horrific aspects of the crime and aimed to minimise their own involvement in the torture and murder.

Due to the way in which the group had disposed of the body, and because there was no way to tell the actual cause of death, the jury couldn't say that Fan's death was murder. As well as this, the defence for the criminals stated that Fan could easily have died of a drug overdose, as she was a known user.

A lesser charge of manslaughter was given to the trio, which sees them able to apply for parole after 20 years.

The 20 years is up this year.

Horrifying True Crime Case #10: James Patterson Smith

The murder of a young woman named Kelly Anne Bates by her boyfriend, James Smith. Smith told police that his teenage girlfriend had accidentally drowned, but in reality, he'd kept her hostage inside his house for weeks and tortured her until she eventually died.

James Smith, an unemployed divorcee from Manchester, UK, was well known for his violent tendencies towards women. His 10-year marriage ended in 1980 because he was physically abusive towards his wife and he would also go on to abuse his next girlfriend, 20-year old Tina Watson. Described as being her 'punching bag,' Smith would even beat her while she was pregnant with his child. At one point, as the young woman was bathing, he forced her head underwater and tried to drown her. Watson managed to flee the abusive relationship, but not before enduring countless outbursts of sadistic violence.

Then, in 1982, Smith entered a relationship with a 15-year old. Due to her young age, his relationship with Wendy Mottershead is classed as statutory rape, although this didn't put the much older man off seeking a relationship with the teenage girl. The teenager, much like Smith's other conquests, would also be subjected to bouts of violence and aggression - he even dunked and held her head underwater in the kitchen sink, which somewhat mirrored his attack on his ex, Tina Watson.

Almost a decade later in 1993, Smith yet again began another relationship with an underage girl. Her name was Kelly Bates and she was only 14-years-old when she was introduced to Smith. Described as bubbly and 'mature for her age', Kelly was your typical teenager. Her parents had brought her up to be independent and self-assured as they had confidence issues growing up and didn't want their daughter to suffer the same difficult childhood. Kelly did her best to conceal the relationship from her parents, who knew about her boyfriend but were unaware of his real age and background - in fact, Kelly even lied about Smith's real name and told her parents he was called 'Dave'. The teenager was reluctant to let her parents meet her first boyfriend, so Margaret asked neighbours and locals about a 32-year old called Dave Smith in an attempt to find out more about who her daughter was caught up with. As you'd expect, Margaret turned up nothing, as a 'Dave Smith' in his early thirties didn't exist in the local area.

After two years of dating, Kelly eventually let her parents meet her partner as she announced she was leaving school and moving in with him. Her parents were dead against this idea, and her mother even enlisted the help of social services to stop her daughter moving out. However, UK law stated that due to Kelly's age - 16 at this point - they were unable to do anything to prevent her from making her own choice in the matter. Powerless to stop their daughter dropping out of education and moving in with her boyfriend, Margaret and Tommy insisted they meet the man their daughter would be living with. They were shocked at what they were confronted with - this man was clearly nowhere near 32 years of age. At 48, he was older than Kelly's dad was at the time.

Despite being mature for her age, Kelly was still a teenager and very naive. The young girl was flattered by Smith's attention and was caught up in the whirlwind of her first romance, and was unaware that the grips of control and coercion were tightening around her neck. It didn't take Smith long at all to begin controlling everything about Kelly's life. Slowly but surely, her demeanour changed. The bright-eyed and bubbly girl was soon replaced with a troubled appearance, and she was showing signs of depression. Margaret and Tommy were gradually seeing less and less of their daughter, and when she did return home, they could see that something was up, but Kelly adamantly denied that anything was wrong. Before long, she was showing up with nasty looking bruises on her face and body. Her parents' worry was brought to a new level when she turned up to their house one day with one side of her face completely black with bruises. There was no way of passing this off as accidental or blaming it on her own clumsiness - you could clearly see that Kelly's face had been pummelled by fists or a weapon. However, as usual, Kelly had a lie ready-made to explain the bruises; she said she was jumped by a group of girls who all beat her up. Because Kelly lied about the age and name of her abusive partner, her parents hadn't been able to discover Smith's history of violence towards women, particularly young women, when they tried to do some digging.

Sadly, even if they *had* discovered his dark past, they were somewhat powerless to help Kelly as she was in the clutches of an abusive relationship and unlikely to leave - even if they physically tried to make her do this. It would probably only have served to push her closer to her abuser. Add to the fact that she was 16 and considered an adult, Margaret and Tommy could do nothing but monitor the situation and be there for their daughter when she needed them.

Regardless of not knowing anything about Smith's past, or who he was as a person, Kelly's parents knew he was bad news. Margaret called the police when her daughter showed up covered in bruises yet again, and they advised she set up a doctors appointment so the abuse could be documented. However, this would be of little help; Kelly was legally an adult, so she couldn't be forced to attend the appointment. Yet again, Kelly showed up to her parent's house with a nasty bite mark on her arm. This would be explained away by Kelly as having caught her arm on a chain-link fence. Of course, her parents weren't blinded by the fibs she was telling, and in November of 1995, Margaret begged her daughter to leave Smith. This had the unintended effect of angering the teenager, and she snapped back at her mother that she would be seeing much less of her moving forward. Heartbreakingly, this would be the last time Margaret would ever see her daughter alive.

Despite their disagreement over her choice of partner, Kelly did maintain some phone contact over the following months. She called to tell her mother that she had got a job at a factory, and was working weekends and long hours, which explained her absence from the family home in recent months.

Eventually, even the phone calls stopped altogether and the Bates family had no contact with their daughter. Heartbroken, but unable to force Kelly to come home, Margaret and Tommy simply waited for their daughter to get back in touch when she was ready. In March 1996, they received a Mother's Day card and a birthday card for Tommy; their relief at hearing from Kelly soon turned into confusion when they opened their cards to see they weren't written in Kelly's handwriting. Smith clearly had taken control of everything, even down to writing out birthday cards. Her parents despaired, convinced that conniving Smith was playing with them and dangling his control of their daughter over their heads. The couple felt frustrated, upset, but most of all, helpless.

The following month, a man calmly walked into Gorton Police Department to report that his girlfriend had drowned in their bathtub. The man was James Patterson Smith.

Kelly was discovered by police when they arrived at his address and headed to the bathroom where he claimed the teen had died. However, the scene they walked into was much more than an accidental drowning - it was a bloodbath. He told the truth about one thing - Kelly had drowned. But that was as far as his honesty went. The state of Kelly's lifeless body told the horrifically violent story of the three weeks leading up to her death.

She'd had her eyes gouged out while she was still alive and there were nasty stab wounds inside her eye sockets. Her eyes had been savagely removed at least a week before she died. The same type of mutilation was discovered inside of her mouth, ears, nose and genitalia. Smith had left her partially scalped. Her knees had been kicked in so she was immobile, unless she crawled - but, without sight, she won't have been able to get far. He scalded her with boiling hot water, burned her with a hot iron, and cut her with various implements including pruning shears. Blood was everywhere - not a room in the house was free of Kelly's spilt blood - and she'd been tied to the radiator by her hair to further stop her from escaping and holding her in place while the torture was being carried out. She'd been starved of food and water, losing around forty-five pounds throughout her ordeal. The emotional suffering and physical pain she would have been in during the last three weeks of her life is unimaginable.

How Smith thought he could get away with passing this off as an 'accidental drowning' is anyone's guess; perhaps he thought police were as empty-headed and lamebrained as he was and wouldn't put the (blatantly obvious) pieces of the macabre puzzle together. It didn't take long for investigators to notice Smith's abusive pattern of behaviour, and statements from his exes would paint him as the controlling, violent, abusive monster he was. He'd tried to drown ex-girlfriends before, and this time he'd succeeded - but not before acting out his wicked reign of terror and torture over his teenage victim.

Smith would show no remorse for his sick actions; on the contrary, he would blame Kelly for the torture she endured as well as her untimely death. He claimed that Kelly provoked him, taunted him about the death of his mother and dared him to gouge her eyes out, to which he obliged. He further blamed her by saying she had a "habit of hurting herself to make it look worse on me," in an apparent attempt to suggest Kelly had inflicted some of the injuries upon herself.

At the trial, the jury needed less than one hour to come up with their guilty verdict. The evidence presented at the trial, alongside the disturbing and graphic pictures of Kelly, was so sickening that the jury were all offered counseling after the trial ended. Every single one of the jury accepted.

Smith was handed life in prison and never expressed any guilt, remorse or sorrow for his vile actions. Kelly was buried the day before she would have turned eighteen.

Horrifying True Crime Case #11: Reynhard Singha

An Indonesian man who was dubbed Britain's worst rapist after he drugged and sexually assaulted up to 190 victims in his Manchester apartment.

"He's effeminate, he's only 5ft 7ins tall, medium build and doesn't come across as threatening," a detective said after capturing mature student Reynhard Singha for drugging and raping men in the Manchester City area. After interviewing him, police said he showed no remorse or sympathy for his victims, and that he seemed sociopathic; one even said he seemed to be enjoying the experience and answering "no comment" to every question directed at him.

The softly-spoken Indonesian certainly isn't your stereotypical image of a serial rapist or sex offender. Small, quiet, well-presented and from a respectable family, Singha was the last person you'd expect to be capable of committing nearly 200 rapes and sexual assaults, which might be why he was able to get away with it for so long.

Born in Jambi, a province of Indonesia, in February 1983, Singha grew up in a wealthy and highly conservative family. His father was a banker, a career that paid enough for the family to comfortably send their son to International School and then across to the UK to study. Singha's student visa brought him to Manchester in 2007 where he would study sociology, then move on to do a PhD in human geography at Leeds University. While studying at Leeds, he stayed in Manchester and commuted to the city in order to attend classes. It appeared Singha had found his home in the city of Manchester.

Singha enjoyed studying, if only because it kept him from having to go back to Indonesia. He told his friends that he wanted to stay in the UK as long as he possibly could, which could have had a lot do to with his sexuality; his family were highly conservative and unlikely to accept the fact he was gay. The thesis he was working on at the time of his arrest may also attest to this also; it was called *'Sexuality and Everyday Transnationalism in South Asian Gay and Bisexual Men in Manchester'.* His love for studying and for the city of Manchester may have simply boiled down to it allowing him to express his sexuality. Studying kept him in Manchester, which in turn allowed him to frequent the plentiful gay bars and be part of a scene that welcomed him in. Singha's youthful looks, unassuming demeanour and his integration in the student community meant that no-one viewed him as a threat. He used this to his advantage to seek out vulnerable, drunken men on nights out. He would befriend them, seek common interests and then invite them back to his flat, to which plenty of drunken young men would oblige - after all, Singha was friendly, too small to be viewed as a threat and the promise of continuing a party sounds good when you're intoxicated.

If you walk through Manchester's bustling Victorian city centre on an evening and head through the abundance of trendy bars, shops and cafes, moving closer to the old textile warehouses, you will be able to hear the music of the Gay

Villiage. Vibrant, full of buzz and a big part of the city's nightlife, the Gay Villiage is a popular area for locals and visitors alike regardless of sexuality. If you walk from here for a few minutes you'll get to Factory Nightclub, above which are rented apartments. One of these properties was rented by Singha's parents for the 36-year-old student to stay at while he earned his doctorate. It was in this flat that the sexual predator drugged and raped at least 190 men. That figure, although not precise, comes about because Singha filmed these attacks. The real figure could well be much higher.

His last victim woke up mid-attack and fought back, beating Singha until he laid limp on the floor. The bravery of the 18-year-old who subdued his sex attacker no doubt put an end to the rapists' spree, which would have very likely continued otherwise. The man was identified as Peter, and although no last name has been given for him to conceal his identity, he spoke with the press about the ordeal he endured on that June evening in 2007.

Unwittingly dosed up on GHB that was slipped into his drink, Peter blacked out at Singha's flat where he'd accepted an invitation to sleep on the floor. Like most of Singha's victims, Peter was heterosexual. It would seem that this was a preference for the rapist, as a way to feel more power and control over his unwitting prey.

Peter recalled, "I woke up disoriented, face down on a pillow. My pants and jeans were down to the top of my knees. He was on top of me with his pants down to his ankles." As Peter groggily awoke from his drug-induced slumber, he slowly realised what was happening to him. Singha retaliated by yelling, "Intruder! Intruder!" and attacking his dazed victim by headbutting him on the nose and biting him. It seems the serial rapist may have pre-planned what his defence would be should any of his victims wake up mid-attack - *he would play the victim*. Although confused, Peter's survival instinct kicked in and he fought back his attacker.

"He was a scrawny little guy," remembers Peter, "I was stronger. I hit him a few times and he dropped to the floor. I was feeling scared. I knew I was in Manchester but that's about it". He added that he thought he may have killed Singha during the fight, unsure of what he was doing but knowing he needed to survive. Peter then fled the flat with Singha's phone in his pocket - if he'd not left with the phone, there's no way to know if the police would ever have even suspected the small, unassuming man of ever being criminal at all, never mind a serial rapist. When Peter called the police, they initially locked *him* up for the assault of Singha, not believing his story. Thankfully, he'd taken the phone that had hundreds of incriminating videos on there of Singha raping unconscious men, including the rape he'd carried out on Peter mere hours before. After 11 hours in a police cell for assault, Peter was eventually released. However, Peter maintained that he still wasn't fully believed until the police searched Singha's phone - in fact after he told them he thought he'd been raped, they didn't test him until two days later. He also states that he was questioned as an offender instead of a victim, and was told that Singha was in the hospital and wouldn't be questioned until he was out. That changed when police uncovered the incriminating videos of hundreds of sexual assaults committed by Singha and filmed with his iPhone.

Police were tasked with identifying all of the men in these videos and getting in touch with them. Singha had even kept some of their personal belongings as trophies - watches, ID cards and even their phones. They used these items to help identify a number of the men who Singha had raped. They managed to obtain dozens of testimonies in court from Singha's victims, the majority of whom were straight and had no idea they'd been violated by the 'good samaritan' Singha portrayed himself as after the attacks he carried out on them. Many of Singha's victims said they didn't recall ever meeting him, even when the police approached them several years later. They were determined that they were barking up the wrong tree until they were shown their faces from stills taken from the videos.

One victim told how he was waiting outside of a nightclub for his girlfriend and was approached by a "small Asian guy". He said the man offered him up to his flat to wait for his girlfriend, where he took a shot of alcohol. After this, the man blacked out. A similar story was recounted by most of the men who testified.

Another explained how his phone had died and Singha invited him up to his flat so he could charge it and "have a quick chat". After giving the victim a false sense of security by having a friendly conversation in his flat, Singha offered the man a drink

- he accepted, then blacked out until the next day. As soon as he woke, he left, unsure of his whereabouts or what had happened. Like almost every other victim, this man had no idea he'd been raped until police told him.

The evidence against Singha was overwhelming; hundreds of hours worth of footage recorded on his phone led police to believe he's been offending for over 10 years. At his trial, Singha sat - often flashing smiles - between three big security guards. The guards towered over the small man with thick-rimmed glasses, who would occasionally play with the shoulder-length hair he'd grown since his arrest. Singha looked almost intrigued as the plethora of nervous young men headed to the witness box to testify against him.

Reporters present at Sinaga's four trials noted that he often seemed to be enjoying himself. They said he could be seen cocking his head to one side as he watched the videos of himself raping dozens of men who'd headed back to his flat after a drunken night out. The sick recordings were made on two separate iPhones, one was perched on his dresser for long shots and the other was handheld. Surprisingly, the videos weren't played as part of his prosecution; it was used for his defence. Singha hoped to show the jury that these men were playing a sexual game with him in the videos.

He insisted that he wasn't the sexual predator he was being made out to be, but rather a harmless deviant. He maintained that he was attractive to young (usually) straight men, who would indulge him in his sexual fantasy where they'd pretend to be asleep and Sinaga would rape them on camera, with some assaults going on for hours. I'm unsure if Singha ever thought this defence would work, or if he simply wanted the videos to be played in court as his final act of humiliation and control.

There was no remorse. Singha insisted that it was a mutual fetish being acted out; a sort of 'underground' sex. The court saw through his lies and eventually convicted him of 136 counts of rape, 14 of sexual assault, eight of attempted rape and another count of assault by penetration In the first two trials he was given 88 concurrent life sentences. After the trial, detectives set up a hotline for victims of Singha, with the expectation that dozens of previously unknown victims could come forward. Imprisoned at HM Prison Manchester, Singha has since refused to cooperate with investigators.

He will be 66 when he is first eligible for release.

***

Thank you for reading *Horrifying True Crime Stories: Book 1*. I know it's not a light read, but if you're anything like me, learning about the horrifying reality of the evil in this world isn't something I want to shut my eyes to or pretend doesn't happen. The crimes outlined in this book are beyond what most of us can comprehend, both from a victim and perpetrator point of view. The thought of enduring the kinds of hell the victims in this book went through is almost impossible - the sheer terror they must have felt in their last moments, the pain and suffering they faced and the evil they were up against is a hard thing to imagine. As for the criminals who carried out the barbaric acts I've talked about, there's no way we can ever truly see through their eyes. The question we all ask but rarely get the answer is '*why*'. As we try to comprehend how another human being could be so cruel and evil, we seek out answers so we can rationalise it in our heads, but most of the time, it's an unachievable endeavour. For some, we can touch on the 'why's' - Edmund Kemper, for example, killed women because he was emotionally and physically abused by his mother. When he killed, he was essentially killing his mother over and over again (which he eventually did in the end). Aileen Wuornos, who had a childhood of abuse and rape, killed men after she was raped and beaten horrifically by one of the men who picked her up for sex. Her life was so complex and damaged that we can delve into her past and somehow find the triggers to her crimes and the possible 'why's'. Not to *excuse* their behaviour, but at least try to *explain* it.

However, with the murderers and abusers in this book, it's hard to answer the question, *'why?'* After researching every perpetrator, I couldn't find anything that made me sympathise with them; no childhood trauma, no true motive other than a lust for wanting to brutally inflict pain on the innocent. They did it because they wanted to; because they wanted to hurt and control another being and play God with their lives. To me, that's evil.

If you liked this book, found out about an interesting case you'd not heard of or are intrigued by the macabre nature of some human beings, please let me know. If you have any ideas for future books, feedback, or true crime stories of your own, then sign up for the newsletter and I'll be in touch.

Also, if you enjoyed this book, it would help me immensely if you left me a rating or a review (and I'd be immensely grateful). The more of these I have, the more visible the book becomes in searches and the more books I'm able to write (and I love writing these books).

Thank you for choosing this book and an even bigger thank you for taking the time to read it. Once again, I hope you enjoyed it.

Remember, you can sign up to my newsletter for more stories of murder and mayhem sent straight to your inbox, plus updates on new books: **https://bit.ly/2zsaUup**

Don't miss out!

Visit the website below and you can sign up to receive emails whenever Danielle Tyning publishes a new book. There's no charge and no obligation.

https://books2read.com/r/B-A-TUJL-WGIJB

BOOKS 2 READ

Connecting independent readers to independent writers.

Did you love *Horrifying True Crime Stories*? Then you should read *Killer Children: Horrifying True Stories of Kids Who Kill*[1] by Danielle Tyning!

When you think about the evil in the world, you conjure up images of those who prey on children, serial murderers, and criminals who carry out sickening and violent acts towards the weak, vulnerable, and undeserving. Names like Bundy, Gacy, and Gein come to mind, alongside the many other murderous

---

1. https://books2read.com/u/bwd1ZZ

2. https://books2read.com/u/bwd1ZZ

people out there who've gained notoriety because of their evil. When you're envisioning the unthinkable and heinous acts that are carried out in this world, it's unlikely you imagine a youngster as being a perpetrator of evil.

Killer children, although rare, do exist. The thought alone is terrifying; we see children as being vulnerable and pure, which makes it harder to comprehend them wanting to inflict pain and suffering on another being. The correlation of a child and unthinkable acts of murder is undeniably tricky to compute.

The children in this book carried out acts of savage murder - even just typing that sentence feels wrong. Some of these murders are sexually motivated; some are carried out for revenge; others are part of an occult ritual. Regardless of the motivation for these children to commit unspeakable acts of cruelty, they are all disturbing.

This book was written to give you some food for thought, to allow you to digest some of the heinous crimes committed by youngsters and consider why they'd carry out such horrific acts. This book will open up a world of questions, many of which I've likely pondered upon myself. While I do offer up my own opinion throughout this book, I do need to (as much as possible) stick to the facts to let you make your own mind up.

With that in mind, let's delve into some of the despicably horrific murders that were carried out by children.

Printed in Great Britain
by Amazon

41445526R00059